HSC

FOR GROWING
FLOWERS
IN THE
Midwest

Pamela Wolfe

CHICAGO
REVIEW
PRESS

*For Andrea and Meredith,
whose gardens are a place to grow
and flowers bloom for me
year-round*

**Library of Congress
Cataloging-in-Publication Data**

Wolfe, Pamela.
   200 tips for growing flowers in the
Midwest / Pamela Wolfe.   -- 1st ed.
       p.   cm.
   Includes index.
   ISBN 1-55652-177-4 (pa) : $6.95
   1. Flower gardening--Middle West.
   2. Perennials--Middle West. I. Title.
II. Title: Two hundred tips for growing
flowers in the Midwest.
SB405.W85   1993
635.9'0977--dc20   92-44584
                                      CIP

Copyright © 1993 by Pamela Wolfe
First Edition
Published by Chicago Review Press,
Incorporated
814 North Franklin Street
Chicago, Illinois 60610

1 2 3 4 5 6 7 8 9 10
ISBN 1-55652-177-4
Printed in the United States of America

CONTENTS

INTRODUCTION

❀ ❀ ❀

With today's busy schedules, the luxury of reading detailed volumes on any subject of interest is a luxury denied. I compiled these accessible, "user friendly" tips to bridge the gap between floundering alone and leisurely researching the world of gardening.

Gardening conditions vary widely in the Midwest. Areas include temperate deciduous forests, wide ranges of temperate grasslands called prairies, and a mixture of the areas in between. The shift from biome to biome is gradual but definite. A variation in rainfall is one mark of difference from one region to another. As the average rainfall decreases and becomes more erratic, the forest landscape changes to grassland. Grassland plants sink deep roots into heavy clay soil, grabbing and holding the water supply as rainfall tapers off. Plants native to forests often perform poorly in areas of low annual rainfall and dense, clay soils.

Temperatures in both midwestern forests and grasslands fluctuate widely. In some spots the swings may go from -45° F in the winter to well over 100° F in the summer. Often the cold snap or midwinter thaw occurs over just a few days or weeks. Grasslands tend to exhibit the widest fluctuations, but all through the Midwest, the range in temperatures makes gardening an adventure in stress management.

A successful, serious gardener knows the climate, soil, and invading weeds of the region. To garden means to work with, to manage, and to interact with the environment. A beautiful, productive garden is part of a process and shows on the gardener as much as on the land. Study, experimentation, and interaction with experienced gardeners should all go together. I am pleased to share the nuggets of my experience with you in these tips.

My sincere appreciation goes to Jim Schuster, Senior II Educator, Horticulture from the Cooperative Extension Service of the University of Illinois at Urbana-Champaign, for the hours of his expert technical editing, and to Mary M. Walker, former Horticulture

Chairman and current Chairman of the Gardening Study Group of the Garden Club of Illinois for the hours she spent on her critique of my ideas, and to all the gardeners I have had the pleasure of knowing. One good gardening friend is worth several reference books.

BEGINNING AT THE GROUND LEVEL

❀ ❀ ❀

Soil

| 1 | An ideal garden soil has the texture of a bag of potting soil. If you are planting that delicate, expensive perennial you've always wanted, don't transplant it into hard ground. Few plants, even indigenous ones, grow well in subsoil. In the Midwest subsoil, though sometimes sand, is usually predominantly clay. It lacks humus

1

or organic matter and grows only the most tenacious weeds. Before you plant one plant, amend at least 5 gallons of soil until it crumbles easily in your hand.

| 2 | **Organic matter such as leaves and manure improves clay soil.** Two-thirds organic matter to one-third clay makes a friable soil. Leaves and compost continue to decay in the ground, releasing valuable nitrogen and phosphorus. As the organic matter continues to decompose, the volume of compost in the soil shrinks. For this reason it may seem impossible to add enough composted leaves and wood chips alone to change the character of true hardpan subsoil. If the proportions seem hard to figure, just keep adding lots!

| 3 | **For soil with truly heavy clay, you must add either sand alone or sand combined with compost.** Just over one half a cubic yard of sand will successfully amend the soil for a planting area of 3-feet by 3-feet wide and 18-inches deep.

The resulting proportions will be about one-third clay to two-thirds sand. Although changing the soil of an entire bed provides the best over-all drainage, you can start small by changing the soil for one group of plants at a time.

4 **If your garden is in a new subdivision, or you've just moved into a newly built home, add copious amounts of sand or sand and peat (some kind of organic matter) to the soil.** Topsoil is removed during the construction of a new home, and this results in a less productive subsoil, which requires amending in order to garden successfully. The subsoil that is left is simply not as fertile as topsoil. A soil profile, a vertical look at a section of soil, shows these layers clearly. Topsoil is the dark layer rich with decayed organic matter. Subsoil is a lighter underlayer.

5 **Work the amended soil so it is raised slightly above the surrounding compacted soil.** Loose soils surrounded by compacted soils may fill with water during heavy rains. Water runs into the amended soil faster than compacted soils allow the water to drain out. Raising the bed will provide some surface drainage. If the hole does fill with water, some of the roots will be above the standing water. Roots down in the waterlogged hole will likely rot.

6 **Beds built even 4 inches above the surrounding soil drain more efficiently than beds level with the ground.** I find slightly raised beds drain quickly and let me garden earlier in the spring. Raising the bed 2 to 3 feet gives the easiest access without relinquishing the advantage of increased soil. Don't make the bed too high. Raised clay soil is still clay soil, and water doesn't move quickly through clay. Many midwestern beds raised above 4 feet with their rich, clay loam drain as slowly as level beds. Add generous quantities of organic matter to the soil used as the growing medium in these beds.

7 Replenishing the soil with a dressing of compost each year will help your garden stay vigorous. Even in the most fertile regions of the Midwest, only good soil husbandry maintains a vibrant garden. A garden stripped of organic matter year after year gradually declines. The soil loses nutrients and the soil structure breaks down. The inclusion of humus (compost) in the spring or fall keeps the soil vital and replenishes flower gardens. A general-purpose fertilizer supplements soil nutrients but can never serve as a substitute for compost in the overall improvement of soil texture and water-holding capacity.

Nutrients

8 In order to choose the correct fertilizer, learn how the major plant nutrients affect plant growth. Plants must receive sufficient amounts of sixteen elemental nutrients. Plants use three of these nutrients—nitrogen, phosphorus, and potassium—in large doses. These are called major nutrients. Every container of fertilizer must prominently record the amount of these three substances. Nitrogen, phosphorus, and potassium are listed as percentages of the bag weight. They are always listed in the same order on the bag—Nitrogen, Phosphorus, and Potassium. Nitrogen stimulates lush green, vegetative growth. Phosphorus encourages root, flower, and hence fruit production. Potassium supports cell development, general health, and disease-fighting capabilities.

| 9 | **Don't over-fertilize plants.** Granular fertilizers contain concentrated fertilizer salts like ammonium nitrate, ammonium sulfate, or potassium sulfate. Usually these products contain more salts than do composted or naturally derived materials. If these salts settle on the leaves, they can dehydrate areas, causing the tissue to die. Also, avoid doses greater than 2 pounds per 100 square feet. Using 10-10-10 at higher rates tends to draw water out of the roots by osmosis. The effect for the plant is equivalent to feeding it potato chips, ice cream, or pizza—it's going to get very thirsty.

10 To avoid burning or drying out plants, compost fresh manures for one year. Animal manure is an excellent source of nitrogen as well as of other minor nutrients. Fresh bird, sheep, and cow manures have the most nutrients. Although manure contains an abundance of nitrogen and micronutrients, fresh manure quickly builds to toxic levels in the soil. Having said this, I must add that I and many of my friends have spread a thin layer—of about 1 inch—of fresh rabbit and guinea pig manure without toxic effects. Actually, adding weed seeds may be a bigger problem when applying fresh horse manure to the garden.

11 Particularly if you are starting a garden in a new subdivision or beside a newly built home, test the pH of the soil. As with a fertilizer analysis, testing for pH indicates how to amend the soil. The acidity and alkalinity of a soil determines the plant's ability to take up nutrients. If the pH is not in a range suited for the plant to take up the substance, it will grow as if the

nutrient were lacking in the soil.
Most plants grow best with a slightly
acid pH, usually around 6.5 to 6.8.
Exceptions are azaleas and rhodo-
dendrons, which require a pH of
about 4.5 to 5.5. Many parts of the
Midwest have soils with a pH above
7.

12 Before adjusting your soil's
pH, call your county extension office. County agents, advisers,
or educators from the land grant university in your state or master gardeners trained by them give accurate
and up-to-date advice for your region. They are aware of local soil
conditions and may be able to inter-
pret soil test results. Becoming familiar with your extension office gives
you a pipeline to specific gardening
advice for your region. Also, any soil
amendment they recommend should
be worked into the soil 6 to 8 inches
deep.

Mulch

13 During the summer a 2- to 4-inch layer of mulch — such as cocoa bean hulls, mushroom compost, rotted hay or straw, or grass clippings — helps conserve water during dry summer stretches, as well as curb the growth of weeds. The mulch traps moisture underneath and slows evaporation. Weed seeds won't usually sprout under a layer of organic mulch. Although very vigorous weeds will grow through mulch, most weeds are smothered by mulch. Roots from weeds that do root in this lighter top layer are easier to pull out than those securely anchored in the ground.

14 A mulch insulates the soil against swings in temperature. The midwestern climate can swing 50 to 60° F in a 24-hour period. A winter night may be 20° F followed by day temperatures close to 70° or even 80° F. Particularly in the spring and fall, a week of 70°-weather followed by a week of consistent 20°-

temperatures affects soil temperature severely. Soil temperature extremes are moderated by a layer of winter mulch. The temperature of the soil will cool and warm more slowly under such a blanket.

15 │ **Nitrogen fertilizer added to a fresh wood chip mulch prevents the yellowing of plants.** A layer of uncomposted woodchips or sawdust depletes soil nitrogen as it decays. To supplement the soil add 1 pound of nitrogen per 1000 square feet of area mulched. Sprinkle the slow-release garden fertilizer before putting down the mulch. Organic sources of nitrogen such as blood meal or fish meal, which can draw rodents, serve the same function as inorganic nitrogen sources. More soluble nitrogen fertilizer can be used to water plants as yellowing of lower leaves occurs.

16 │ **If you can get it, mushroom compost is both an effective mulch and a very good source of humus or organic matter.** In this way, the soil will be replenished as

the plants are being mulched. In the Midwest you may find local industries that have processing plants for organic materials like soy beans, corncobs, and hay. Spreading any of these on the soil as a mulch works well.

17 **Mulch the perennial beds for winter with leaves raked or blown from the yard.** Although locust or ash leaves are unlikely to need further chopping, large leaves like maple, sycamore, and sometimes even oak tend to mat down when they are wet and smother the garden. Mow over leaves before raking them onto the garden. The chopped leaf litter raked directly onto the garden makes a winter mulch that is less likely than larger leaves to mat down. As the winter proceeds the small pieces decay more rapidly than larger ones added to the organic matter of the soil.

18 **After mulching a bed for winter, try adding branches found lying around the yard.** The leaves nestle against them and blow around less. I particularly find that evergreen branches left over after Christmas make a very effective additional protective layer of insulation. In early spring, as the ground thaws, I take the branches off and pull the leaves aside with my hands. This exposes the growing crowns. I don't remove the leaves entirely from the beds. They seem to disintegrate in place before I get the chance.

19 Sand, loose soil, or finely ground leaves work well to insulate plants from rapid and continuous freezing and thawing. Any material that is porous will drain rapidly and not freeze on top of plant like a block of ice. Covering this layer with wood chips and fresh manure gives a final layer of insulation. The slightly heavier top layer helps hold leaves in place. Remove the layers slowly, pulling them back from the centers of the plants as growth begins.

20 Plants like primroses, poppies, some iris, and any others that retain top growth all win-

ter should have mulch tucked in only around their crowns. Put only the lightest covering over their tops. Heavy, wet mulch can so easily rot their crowns. In the early spring, begin to remove organic mulches from the crowns of primroses earlier than from plants that go completely dormant.

| 21 | **Don't remove winter mulch too early.** I have had more plants die in March and April than in midwinter. When the winter leaves are first removed or blow off too early, the plant can look just as it did in the fall. But after a few dips in temperature and some sharp cold winds, the next time I look at the plant it is dead. I don't think mulch should be taken off until the soil has thawed completely. After the mulch is off, the soil will warm quickly and growth will take off. In the early spring, premature growth may mean premature freezing—with devastating results. When it is warm and sunny, you may spend a joyful day completely cleaning off your beds.

Compost

22 **Compost adds organic matter to the soil.** Since organic matter enriches subsoil and creates topsoil, compost benefits the garden. Both sandy and clay soils are improved. Compost increases the pore size of clay soil, promoting drainage and making it more crumbly. Compost acts to hold sandy soil together, improving its water-holding capacity. Although it sounds contradictory to say that organic matter can improve drainage *and* help water-holding capacity, compost does just that. A heavy clay soil and a light sandy soil will both be more friable with the addition of compost.

23 **Composting directly into the ground skirts keeping a compost pile.** Leaves, grass clippings, and other organic debris piled directly into a hole in the ground serve the same purpose as a compost pile and help to amend the soil in that spot. Dig a hole about 18 inches deep and fill it with fresh or dried organic matter. Mounding it slightly is fine.

Cover the top with 2 to 3 inches of soil. A stepping stone on top marks the spot. As the material decays, the soil will settle. In 6 to 12 months, plant directly into the spot or harvest the compost.

| 24 | **If you don't use grass clippings in your compost pile, add 2 inches of manure or just under a cup of nitrogen fertilizer to every 10 inches of leaves or kitchen waste.** In addition to increasing fertility, mixing composted manure into the soil before planting improves soil texture and structure.

| 25 | **Compost piles that are turned regularly, put together with alternating layers of fresh organic matter and soil, and given a balanced fertilizer decompose more quickly than just a heap of yard waste.** A mound of yard waste, unceremoniously piled up, will decay more slowly and leave you with less overall nutrient value by the end. Mulch from either type of pile will improve the texture, structure, and water-holding capacity of

soil. However, the faster the decomposition occurs, the richer in nitrates the mulch will be. Nitrogen compounds wash out of the soil and out of the compost pile rather quickly.

| 26 | **Sprinkling the compost pile speeds decomposition.** The microbes that act to digest the organic matter need water to grow. Since soaking the inside of the pile will speed the downward movement of nitrogen compounds, wet down only the outside of the pile. Using excess water to wash soluble salts such as valuable nitrates out of the soil is called leaching. When watering a compost pile, use enough water to allow the reactions to take place. Excess water results in leaching valuable nutrients out of the soil and slowing decomposition. Keep it just "moist."

DESIGNING YOUR GARDEN

❀ ❀ ❀

Garden Styles

27 **A well-designed garden is more than a collection of flowers.** Put in enough of one cultivar to make an impact. Usually three to five of any one plant keeps an area of the garden from looking busy. Don't be afraid to repeat a flower you like throughout the garden. Repetition creates a kind of movement and visual rhythm. A smooth transition is achieved when shifts in color and texture are made slowly.

Understand which plant, in color and texture, creates emphasis — carries a visual punch — and use just enough of that plant to create the effect you want.

28 **Attending to the details of growth requirements determines a garden's success.** Double- and triple-check the catalog or other reference to find the plant's growing requirements. Although a thoughtfully designed garden produces harmonious results, sacrificing cultural requirements for design considerations results in poor growth if any. A plant's cultural and environmental requirements can not be ignored. Careful attention to details of exposure, slope, and soil determines which plants to use. Studying where the plant grows in a natural habitat helps suggest where it will grow successfully in your garden. A plant native to the mountains won't easily survive a heavy soil and a hot, humid environment.

29 Design the layout of your garden as if you were choosing and positioning flowers for a large flower arrangement. The colors, textures, sizes, and positions of the flowers and leaves should complement each other. Choose a style you like—large, bold overflowing Dutch Master bouquets alive with color and form, the elegantly simple Japanese style with its line and emphasis, or hues of pastels gently softening the landscape. Make it an arrangement that reflects your personality and color preferences.

30 To create an entire garden that is colorful, weave the same plant throughout different beds or places in the landscape. The repeated plant should be one that is exceptionally long flowering or especially appealing. When a particular plant dominates each bloom period, it carries a theme all the way through the garden giving a rhythm and continuity to the garden. At any one time the entire garden will be tied together with the color and form of the particular plant that is blooming or has striking foliage. Every few weeks the color may change like a wave sweeping across your entire garden.

---

31 A permanent structure, like a decorative rail fence running down the center of a bed, becomes the utilitarian midwestern equivalent of garden sculpture. The vertical structure creates interest during the winter when snow piles on the posts and rails. During the growing season the fence is the backdrop and visual anchor for the garden. Climbing vines like clematis, which cannot possibly wind gracefully through the branches of trees as they do in milder climates, drape themselves lazily along the fence. The fence is made more interesting as plants grow up and conceal it or die back to reveal it.

---

32 Don't choose a plant just for its flowers. In the Midwest few seasons linger. Most flowers bloom later and for a shorter period of time than in the gardening meccas of the world. When plants bloom, many literally explode and in only days are gone. But plants like iris form clumps of sword-like leaves that contrast with many summer and fall flowering plants. Many shades and texture of green provide a mosaic that can be stunning. *Hosta*, *Bergenia*, *Artemesia*, sea-lavender (*Limonium latifolium*), *Verbascum*, and plume poppy (*Macleaya cordatata*) are grown primarily for their foliage. In addition, many fine flowering plants such as peonies, daylilies, celadine poppies, and irises have the bonus of attractive foliage.

33 **To fine-tune the composition of the garden, walk through the garden in bloom eyeing possible new combinations.** One gardening friend picks a flower and holds it up to possible new companions. Another friend asked and received several daylily blossoms from a nursery to bring home and check out in the garden. The spectrum of peachy, pink, and orange flowers of daylilies often belies their final combined effect. Experimenting directly with the arrangement of different plants lets those that sit close together fit as if they were in a bouquet.

34 Don't make the jump from one extreme in plant form, texture, or color to another without some middle-ground transition. For instance, if you combine Asiatic lilies with baby's breath, add moderating plants like several single-flowering roses, some sundrops (*Oenothera*), or even some snapdragons. Several midsize plants make a smoother visual transition.

35 Gardens appeal to all the senses—even hearing. Rustling of tall grasses in late summer and fall is restful and more delicate than the endless tinny clanging of wind chimes. The sounds of a garden change with the seasons. If you can hear changes in your garden, you have a beautiful spot to track the sounds of the year. Birds are wonderful as they travel through, but overlooked or often looked on with contempt are the sounds of insects. Their gentle buzzing, whirring, clicking livens the air and brings a feeling of wildness.

36 In the early evening, white flowers and variegated plants with white and green foliage light up the garden. The reflective power of white works as well as garden lighting. At night any ambient light travels throughout the garden beds on the white flowers. Plant white in spots to catch late light or to illuminate a dark corner. Because of the intensifying nature of white, avoid it in a candy-cane or alternating pattern with a hot color like red. You'll want white to stimulate the surroundings—not electrify them.

37 Plant bulbs in a group of at least a half a dozen or so for an effective show. Since a mass of yellowing foliage of the spring-flowering bulbs like tulips and daffodils detracts from the late spring and early summer garden, plant seedling annuals in and around a spring-flowering bulb display. The dying foliage shades the newly planted seedlings and gives the foliage time to die back naturally. As long as the foliage is green, it is manufacturing carbohydrates to replenish the bulbs. When leaves yellow, they can be removed with a gentle tug.

| 38 | In a small garden, gradual small changes in elevation can create a sense of space. If the finished bed is slightly raised the garden is easier to maintain. Don't make the rise too great. Subtlety goes a long way in giving the garden an elegant look. When flat spaces are blocked by buildings, panoramic views end. Tricks of elevation and the shapes of beds can create a sense of distance. Opening and closing the space that exists directs the eye to see paths leading to nowhere in particular. Cleverly built small gardens contain a collection of optical illusions that take the place of continuous space and when done well don't look contrived.

Plants to Consider

| 39 | Daffodils are the most widely grown of the spring-flowering bulbs. They range from early blooming varieties, which start in late March or early April, to varieties blooming in late April and early May. The late-blooming daffodils

are the most reliable. Long periods (more than a week) of below freezing temperatures may damage or kill those whose flowers are blooming. A light frost later in the spring will not ruin the whole show so dependably. Tulips are not as constant as daffodils and jonquils (*Narcissus*). They are more frost sensitive and do not return nearly as dependably as daffodils. Animals eat the bulbs and the foliage. A cold, late spring may kill the shoots as they sprout, resulting in distorted plants and flowers.

| 40 | One of the most dependable small, flowering spring bulbs is the Siberian squill (*Scilla*). The deep blue, tiny bell-like blossoms radiate far beyond their size. They easily spread out in the garden by self-seeding. Since the thin, sedge-like leaves die back after they bloom, squill work well in areas of light shade and thin turf. A similar but distinct early beauty, glory-of-the-snow (*Chionodoxa*) gives a welcome preview of spring and spreads easily to colonize an area. The squill survives further north (zone 2), but glory-of-the-snow does well into zone 4.

41 A large group of plants that I'd like to see in more midwestern gardens is the Geranium genus—not to be confused with Pelargonium, the colorful geraniums sold as annuals here. Many will bloom for over a month and the mounding form of their delicately dissected leaves decorates the rest of the growing season. Although many are associated with spring wildflowers, some like the low-growing *Geranium cinereum* bloom throughout most of the summer. In partial shade and moist, well-drained soils they are easy to grow.

42 Fall-flowering anemones (*Anemone x hybrida* and *A. vitifolia*) are dependable in some ways and temperamental in others. In sun or partial shade many flower from August to October. The blooms have a spring-like look. But the beautiful, soft pink of *Anemone vitifolia* 'Robustissima' planted with asters and monarda transcends the seasons. They do best in moist, well-drained soil. They do not transplant easily, but their delightful elegance make them well worth the effort.

43 The colorful, daisy-like, fall-flowering asters deserve to be in more midwestern gardens. They are colorful, dependable, and adaptable. Many native asters along with the showy, hybrid cultivars grow easily, producing attractive patches of pinks and blues in late summer and fall. For many midwestern gardeners, they overwinter more dependably than do chrysanthemums, which seem more widely available. Divide asters frequently, perhaps as often as every year or two, to keep them blooming vigorously. When they bloom poorly, divide them.

44 The celandine poppy (*Stylophorum diphylum*) has the sought-after characteristic of flowering, albeit sparsely, all summer. In addition to that, it has the bonus of thriving in shade—even rather deep shade. I must add that the foliage is fine and soft without being busy. It prefers moist locations, but I have noticed it growing where no extra summer watering occurs. The clear buttercup yellow flowers brighten the shady nooks where I grow it. Since it seems rather vigorous, I am surprised so few growers include it.

| 45 | Ferns offer an interesting texture and a wide range of hue to moist, shadowy areas. Gardens that include ferns evoke woodland glades rich with graceful fronds. The large 4-foot, light green feathers produced by the ostrich fern offer a spectacular sweep. I particularly enjoy the lady fern (*Athyrium*), the Japanese painted fern (*Athyrium*), the toothed wood fern (*Dryopteris*), and the Christmas fern (*Polystichium*). But I can truthfully say I've never met a fern I didn't like. Just check their mature size before blending them into your shady glen.

| 46 | Another low-growing, shade-tolerant plant, Lady's mantle (*Alchemilla*), furnishes puffy clusters of tiny chartreuse flowers. These bunches of small, inconspicuous flowers produce an impressive sight. The very light-yellow green clouds splendidly set off the surrounding early summer flowers. The

grey-green oval leaves are deeply serrated. One of the most striking characteristics is the leaf's tendency to guttate water from the ends of the little teeth along its margin. The morning dew gathers like a necklace of small jewels around its edge, bringing unexpected light to the garden.

47 | **During the entire year, small deciduous flowering shrubs will give your garden form, texture, and color.** The color of their blooms; their leaves in spring, summer, and fall; their bare branches in autumn and winter all create visual interest during the year. They add height and depth to the otherwise herbaceous border. Their permanence gives stability. Their mass gives protection. A few of my favorites: the dwarf *Spirea japonica* 'Little Princess', butterfly bush (*Buddleia alternifolia*), *Hydrangea* 'Annabelle', old-fashioned weigela (*Weigela florida*), Oregon grapeholly (*Mahonia aquifolium*), dwarf fothergilla, the red leaf rose (*Rosa rubrifolia*), and the relatively small, fragrant lilac, 'Miss Kim'.

48 For the unique and delicate effect of clematis, use the more upright, rather bushy forms in the Midwest. Choose among three herbaceous, non-vining forms of clematis: *Clematis heracleifolia*, *C. integrifolia*, and *C. recta*. All of these make effective garden additions with blue or white flowers. *C. heracleifolia* produces clusters of attractive, tubular blue, fragrant flowers in late summer followed by ornate seed pods. *C. integrifolia* grows as a more compact roughly 2-foot, herbaceous plant with striking deep blue-violet blossoms that hang like pendants from slender stems. *C. recta* comes into masses of small, white starry blooms with the spring peonies. As these aren't extremely sturdy, either stake them or let them flop on a fence, along the ground, or over a rock.

49 Landscape roses blend well into a mixed border. Many rose breeders today are blending the best characteristics of old roses with plants that are continuous bloomers, cold-tolerant, disease-resistant, and more compact in size. Names of recent introductions like 'Simplicity',

'Carefree Beauty', 'Bonica', along with names of familiar breeders like Dr. Griffith Bucks of Ames, Iowa, David Austin of Albrighton, England, and House of Meilland in France tell the direction of roses today. Roses that are reliable, disease-resistant, environmentally friendly, energy economic, and gorgeous are more and more common.

The Best Combinations for the Midwest

50 **Mixing daylilies in a perennial bed becomes an alternative to the total monoculture planting.** Today blossoms of daylilies span a wide range of size, form, and color. New cultivars range from the large, ruffled blossoms of tetraploid hybrids to the slender stalks, clustered with miniature flowers. No longer are they invasive, like the common orange daylily, *Hemerocallis fulva*, a native of Eurasia naturalized throughout the Midwest. The newer shades range from pale mint-greenish white of 'Mint Ice' to the rich, chestnut brown of 'Ginger Cookie'.

51 Try blending some daylilies that catch your eye with large patches of the graceful white goose-neck loosestrife (*Lysimachia clethroides*), veronica (*Veronica longifolia* or *V. spicata*), the stately blue globe thistle (*Echinops ritro* 'Taplow Blue'), the delicate blackberry lily (*Belamcanda chinensis*), Russian sage (*Perovskia atriplicifolia*), and a yellow-flowered yarrow (*Achillea* 'Coronation Gold'). The blues, yellows, oranges, and whites of this mix combine to serve as a interesting backdrop for the wide range of daylily choices.

52 The soft pastel shades of purple prairie coneflower (*Echinacea purpurea*), catmint (*Nepeta*), Russian sage (*Perovskia*), moonbeam coreopsis (*Coreopsis verticilla* 'Moonbeam'), variegated hosta, the daylily 'Catherine Woodbury', the shrub rose 'Simplicity', and annual bachelor buttons (*Centaurea cyanus*) come

together with a lush, gentle beauty. This will flourish in spots with full sun to light shade. The subtle pinks, blues, lavenders, and yellows flower from late June through August and when the frost doesn't hit too early even into late September or early October. The colors are eye-catching without the brilliance of more vibrant combinations.

| 53 | It's a challenge, but you can find plants that have a good vertical line. |

The very tall, thin, graceful, white spikes of black snakeroot (*Cimicifuga racemosa*) grow in moist, lightly shaded spots in early July. Pink or white obedient plant (*Physostegia virginiana*) forms a thick, full plant that seems impervious to poor spring weather that may kill more finely rooted plants. The blazing star (*Liatris spicata* 'Kobold') puts out its feathery spikes in sunny spots. Together these bloom in shades of pink, lavender, and white and stand between 3 to 6 feet tall. Their sturdy and upright habit withstands the climate and remains attractive for up to a month in midsummer.

54 A rock garden can be simple. Besides the deliberate areas of boulders and stones, free laid (no cement, just sand) limestone retaining walls, walkways, steps, and terraces serve as functional planting beds. Some of the most reliable rock garden plants in the Midwest include common sea thrift (*Armeria*), creeping baby's breath (*Gypsophilia repens*),dalmation cranesbill (*Geranium dalmaticum*), snow-in-summer (*Cerastium*), candytuft (*Iberis*), various members of the stonecrop family (*Sedum*), hen and chicks (*Sempervivum*), rock cress (*Arabis*), pinks (*Dianthus*), low-growing speedwells (*Veronica prostrata*), and thyme (*Thymus*).

55 Another use of low-growing, surface-rooted plants is as companions to woody flowering plants like the dwarf spireas, small landscape roses, Japanese kerria (*Kerria japonica*), dwarf barberries, slender deutzia, dwarf viburnums, or small hydrangeas. Just a few of the attractive low-growing plants that work well are sweet woodruff (*Galium*), lamb's ear

(*Stachys*), dwarf or star astilbe (*A. simplicifolia*), the low-growing blue bellflower *Campanula carpatica*, or one of the cultivars of *Lamium*. Tucking a few annuals in and around the planting adds an extra lush touch.

56 **Plants traditionally referred to as ground covers will often enhance the appearance of your flower garden.** Many produce lovely, usually small flowers that blanket the ground when they bloom. Sweet woodruff (*Galium odoratum*), myrtle (*Vinca minor*), alleghany spurge (*Pachysandra procumbens*), Japanese spurge (*Pachysandra terminalis*), and various species of sedum come as ground covers rather than perennials for the garden, yet have attractive flowers, beautiful form and foliage, and are evergreen throughout much of the Midwest. Weaving these in areas of the flower garden gives a background as well as a spark of seasonal interest. Count on them as reliable garden plants.

57 In shady areas, the uniform oval, dark, glossy green leaves of the European ginger (*Asarum europaeum*) contrast with the finer textures of fringed bleeding heart (*Dicentra eximia*) and yellow corydalis (*Corydalis lutea*). In protected spots or nearer the tree's trunk, the larger, somewhat evergreen leaves of bergenia look wonderful as a backdrop to the arrangement. Flowers sporadically (some seasons are a wash) rise out of bergenia's broad, wrinkled leaves like hyacinth in shades of red, pink, purple, or white. Although the flowers are attractive and long-lasting, the bold, coarse-textured leaves usually dominate the planting.

58 Turf grasses compete with tree roots, and lawn mowers damage tree trunks—hence the search for attractive "tree-friendly" plants to grow underneath the trees. Many shade-loving plants with attractive flowers and foliage exist. The woodland phlox (*Phlox divaricata*), Virginia bluebells (*Mertensia virginica*), lungwort (*Pulmonaria*), Solomon's seal (*Poly-*

gonatum biflorum or *P. commutatum*),
false Solomon's seal (*Smilacina racemosa*),
primrose (*Primula* x *polyantha*), and
foamflower (*Tiarella cordifolia*) are
just a few of the many flowering
plants that thrive under the canopy.

59 **During late July and August,
the luminous orange clus-
ters of small, succulent blossoms of
butterfly weed (*Asclepias tuberosa*)
and the spherical blue flower buds
of the balloon flower (*Platycodon
grandiflorum*) make a stunning
show.** The balloon flower blossoms
open into 1-inch bright blue bells
near the top of the stems. An overlooked beauty is the fall foliage of the
balloon flower. The upright, 3- to
4-foot clumps turn a bright yellow in
October—one of the best fall color
displays of any perennial's leaves.
The native butterfly weed has a
flower so colorful and delicate that
the most conservative gardeners
look for a spot for it to grow. As with
other milkweeds, it has the added
attraction of luring Monarch butter-
flies.

60 Here is a majestic combination for your Midwest garden: tall blue flowering asters, the mass of tiny white and yellow daisies of 'Snow Bank' boltonia, the erupting streaks of yellow from the golden rods (of which there are many to choose) and the iridescent, almost electric foliage of Artemisia 'Lambrook Silver'. The fall display made by these beauties casts a spell on the quickening days.

61 The native prairie grass big bluestem (*Andropogon gerardi*) and common sneezeweed (*Helenium autumnale*), which does not produce sneezing, make an attractive autumn combination. The graceful clumps of the tall prairie grass rise a foot or two above the range of yellow to mahogany daisy-like flowers of the helenium's stately display. Flowering from August late into the fall, the blend of color, rustling leaves, and thick, lush form is delightful.

62 Don't be afraid to use wildflowers that invade your
garden, but learn to recognize what
you have. Wildflowers like the various daisy fleabanes (*Erigeron*), gold-
enrods (*Solidago*), asters, phlox, or
dame's rocket (*Hesperis matronalis*)
may just appear in your garden. Use
careful management. Some may
need dead-heading to keep them
from spreading like crazy. Others
may be very appealing sweeping
over a large space. For those
which are very aggressive in your
area, rip the whole plant out after
it flowers and before it develops mature seeds.

63 Forget-me-nots (*Myosotis*),
dame's rocket (*Hesperis
matronalis*), and the natives columbine (*Aquilegia canadensis*), perennial verbena (*Verbena canadensis*),
and celandine poppy (*Stylophorum
diphyllum*) are some of my favorite
perennial plants that spread by
seeds. The dry seed pods hold hun-
dreds of potential new plants. Clear
a new site of weeds or lawn and make
sure the soil is soft and well cultivated. By mid- to late summer shake

the mature pods over a new site. A site with one or more trees and moist, forest soil works perfectly for these treasures.

Growing Flowers that Are Not Perennial

64 When you are eager to have a bed overflow with growth, the bare spaces left by spring-flowering bulbs may be disconcerting. Even before the foliage dies back, plant small seedling transplants of short, shallow-rooted annuals like fibrous begonia, ageratum, alyssum, or verbena. Planting a few seeds of portulaca, larkspur, nigella, California poppies, bachelor buttons, or cosmos also will fill in the area without disturbing the bulbs. Chances are most annuals you pick, if they are planted while they are small, won't disturb most spring-flowering bulbs.

65 Attractive, resilient, reseeding annuals bring color and changing interest each year to your rock garden. These plants die each fall, but their seeds remain to sprout in the spring. They may appear in different spots throughout the garden, but will grow vigorously in the Midwest. A short list of low growing returning annuals: the dalberg daisy (*Thymophylla tenuiloba*), sweet alyssum (*Lobularia maritima*), and moss rose (*Portulaca*).

66 In a large flower border, self-sowing annuals will add variety as well as stability to your garden. Plants like cleome, annual larkspur, summer balsam, and cosmos don't survive the winters, but their seeds do. These are tall, striking plants that grow each spring from the seeds of last year's plants. The new plants start flowering in early to midsummer. Cleome, summer balsam, and cosmos will flower until frost. Many self-seeding annuals are more dependable than perennials. Some might say they are weedy. But if you get too many or in the "wrong" spot, they are easy to weed.

67 | I think using self-seeding annuals and perennials requires discipline as well as a willingness to let go. For these plants to mature to their finest glory, they must be thinned. Pulling out plants you've let grow from seeds always takes conviction, especially for the beginner. Be ruthless. The effect of fewer large plants is generally more pleasing than a group of many crowded, stunted ones. But the interesting aspect of these plants is the variety they add to the garden. Allowing the plants to weave around your garden from year to year produces a lush look of carefree abandon. Giving up control of "design" may be difficult, but this technique will make your garden exciting to look at.

68 | Annuals add color where there was none and give continuous color to the garden. In the coldest regions of the country, annuals bring a welcome brilliance to the short sunny summers. Many perennials bloom for only a short time, and annuals link the colors from one

group of perennials and one season of perennials to the next.

| 69 | To give your garden a new and different look, let annuals change each year or two.** Reseeding annuals will do that themselves but even for transplants, choose a different color or put them in a different place. If you always use red geraniums, try pink ones. If you always use white begonias, try vinca. Changing some plants from year to year creates interest. The annuals become less like fixtures or window dressing and much more "alive," piquing curiosity as they grow and develop.

Gardening with Containers

| 70 | Avoid using garden soil directly in containers.** The clay present in most soil compacts easily. The tiny particles clump together when heavily watered, forcing out air spaces. These spaces are lost and the soil dries hard as a brick, strangling

the roots. Add at least two-thirds peat moss or vermiculite. Some microorganisms in soil cause diseases. In the confined space of a pot and the stress that puts on a plant, these pests may become serious problems. Disinfect the soil with heat by putting a clay pot full of moist soil in the oven and heating it until the center of the soil ball is 160° F for thirty minutes. If that seems like a nuisance, buy a seed-starting mixture labeled 'pasteurized' from a garden center.

71 **Plants grown in containers dry out quickly.** If you can actually find ways to prevent wilting, you'll have healthier plants than any amount of catch-up watering will give you after the wilting occurs. After a plant wilts severely, the lower leaves yellow and fall off. Once a plant wilts, it loses the vigor it had before the water stress. The first sign of wilting is a softening of the leaves. Try to water the plant before the stress is irreversible; water just as the turgidity lapses. Adding peat moss to a commercial potting soil improves its capacity to hold water.

72 Most container plants need to be fertilized regularly with a soluble fertilizer. Commercial growing mixes suitable for containers have some combination of peat moss, vermiculite, and perlite or bark. They lack natural nutrients present in soil. Supplement the major plant nutrients—nitrogen, phosphorus, potassium—with any commercial fertilizer about once a week. Organic fertilizers like composted cow manure have a lower amount of major nutrients, but will supply some of the minor nutrients.

73 Any pot without drainage holes is unsuitable for direct planting. Put the plant in a pot with drainage holes and set that container inside the decorative one. Always dump out excess water. Placing stones on the bottom of the decorative pot keeps the roots from becoming saturated. If the roots stay wet, most will die from lack of air. Sometimes decorative pots have a rim holding the plant's pot off of the bottom. This can help keep the plant from sitting in water depending on the height of the rim and how heavily the plant is watered.

74 In the late fall, containers planted with hardy perennial plants should be moved to an area where the plants will not freeze and thaw. Put them in the warmest part of an unheated garage. When possible, bury the containers in loose soil or sand and cover the area with some rapidly draining mulch material. Make sure they freeze as dry as possible. Evergreen branches laid over the plants make an excellent insulating material. Wood chips also drain quickly, making them suitable for winter mulch.

Not the Best Choices for the Midwest Garden

75 Although glorious in the right spot, lupine, delphinium, and foxglove are not for the beginner—especially in the Midwest. At home in the cool summers and loose soils of the most northern stretches of the region, they require work to survive in areas of heavy clay and hot, humid summers. Most of the Midwest's soil is alkaline enough for delphiniums, but they thrive in areas of loose soil and cool, dry air. Since they are short-lived perennials, a plant that survives for five years is an antique. Lupines reseed in the sandy soils of northern Michigan, but are not so vigorous in the clay soils of the southern parts. Even foxglove is not really a perennial, but a biennial. When given the shaded location that many authors suggest, it easily becomes coated with mildew. Don't pick these beauties for your first garden.

| 76 | **Plants that may or may not come back year after year are considered short-lived perennials.** Sometimes the growing conditions kill them, sometimes they are just short-lived. If you want them in the garden, plan to replant them every few years. Coral bells, chrysanthemums, painted daisies, gaillardia, and dianthus are a few favorites that die easily in the wave

action of our winters. But shallow, fibrous-rooted plants are even shorter lived in the Midwest's heavy clay soil. The constant freezing and thawing during early and late winter heave these plants out of the ground. Use deeper, thick-rooted plants like peonies, daylilies, hosta, physotegia, platycodon, achillea, or bergenia, or amend the soil to drain efficiently.

PLANTING YOUR GARDEN

❀ ❀ ❀

Starting Seeds and Transplants

| 77 | **Start seeds indoors using pasteurized soil and con-**
tainers. Fungal and bacterial spores are everywhere, just waiting for the right growing conditions. Any place previously touched by growing or once growing plants holds thousands of these unseen agents. Newly planted seeds sown in previously

used, unpasteurized soil provide certain targets. Buying pasteurized seed starting mixtures cuts down on contamination. Commercial seed-starting mixes are more expensive but more convenient than home prepared ones.

78 **Since growing a perennial plant from seed usually takes more than one season, most beginners plant transplants.** Starting perennials from seed takes patience. By the end of the first season the seedling often grows to a 3- or 4-inch pot. The second year the plant grows to fill a half gallon or gallon container. These larger sizes are the sizes most frequently sold in nurseries. Not all perennials grow easily or true to type from seed. Some are started from cuttings or divisions.

79 **Most perennials take two years to flower from seed.** Shasta daisy 'Snow Lady' and blanket flower *Gaillardia*, as well as hollyhock and purple coneflowers, will flower from seed the first year they are planted. For most perennials

keep the seedlings in small pots or flats in a shaded spot. Mulch them thoroughly during the first winter.

80 **To shorten the growing time some perennials can be seeded in the summer or fall to flower the following spring.** Often a perennial needs a winter in the ground in order to flower. Some like *Campanula*, *Aquilegia*, *Viola*, and *Linum* sown in the fall outdoors in seed beds or in pots protected in cold frames will sprout in the spring. With this treatment, these may even flower the first year.

81 **To overwinter a perennial seedling, prepare a nursery bed or cold frame.** Planting tiny seedlings directly in the garden will work, but the tiny plants are easy to lose in the jungle that sprouts in the spring. During the winter a cold frame keeps the plants from continually and rapidly freezing and thawing. There the small pots remain safely dormant all winter. A separate, carefully labeled seedling bed may serve as an alternative for small developing sprouts.

| 82 | **If you are planting seed indoors, carefully prepare the soil.** The clean, moist seed-starting mix must be absolutely flat and compressed in the container. If not, the light texture of seed-starting media makes a lumpy surface with air pockets that will dry quickly and kill the seeds. Tamp the soil firmly with a small board, chunk of wood, or something smooth. Even taking one tray or pot to press down and smooth the soil of another will work. The soil must be even.

| 83 | Before starting seeds indoors, **moisten the soil to the consistency of a saturated sponge.** Since some seeds have special temperature and light requirements, plant the seeds according to the directions on the packet. After planting don't water the seeds. A stream of water washes the seeds into a pile at the edge of the pot. To slow drying, cover the seeds with something transparent, such as a large plastic

bag or a piece of clear plastic or glass. Make sure the covering has some ventilation holes. If the surface becomes dry, water lightly with a fine mist.

84 **Be most careful not to let the plastic touch the little plants as they sprout.** Any new leaves touching or adhering to the plastic by droplets of water quickly rot. As the leaves get larger and the stems longer, prop open the bag to let in fresh air. This dries the air slowly. Air circulation slows the growth of diseases. The newly forming roots now begin to compensate for the lack of moisture in the air. By the time the second set of leaves appears the plant should be out of the bag.

85 **Most perennial seeds are tiny, so do not cover them with soil.** (They drop between the spaces in the soil anyway.) The rule of thumb is: cover seeds one to two times their largest diameter with soil. If planted too deep, the seed won't grow. If planted at the right depth, each seed carries enough food to

survive until it hits light of day. It won't make it if the food runs out. Planted too shallowly, the seed will tend to dry out. Some seeds are so small that merely sprinkling them on the soil allows them to fall between the crevices of the soil grains. Light is necessary for some seeds to germinate. When in doubt, follow the directions on the packet.

| 86 | To sprout seed and to cut down on the spread of disease, try to establish a difference in temperature between air and soil. When you start seeds indoors, the rate of germination is higher when the soil temperature is slightly warmer than the air temperature. As they grow, keep the seedlings as cool as possible to produce healthier, sturdier plants. When you cannot give them the bright environment of a greenhouse, a cool room with the best light you have grows the best seedlings.

| 87 | When the emerging perennial seedling develops the first set of true leaves, transplant.

If you plant the seeds far enough apart that the emerging seedlings will not crowd each other, you can avoid transplanting. If you do need to transplant, watch for the true leaves, which unfold immediately after the one or two seed leaves. The form of these "true leaves" takes the shape of the leaves of the mature plant. The seed leaves, on the other hand, often have a very different appearance. Waiting too long to transplant the seedling can cause tangled roots, which tear easily, putting the plant in a greater transplant shock.

88 **Damping-off is the most common disease of seedlings started indoors.** Learn what it looks like and how to prevent it. A fungus that grows in soil water causes this disease, which attacks seedlings as soon as they sprout. The little seedling stands there with just its seed leaves and then it falls over—never to get up. When the soil is too wet and lacks enough air, damping-off runs rampant.

89 | Sometimes seedlings with the fungal disease that causes damping-off fall over when watered with a spray bottle or watering can—and they pop back up. The damping-off fungus grows right below the soil level and girdles the stem of the germinating seedling. To prevent this, use pasteurized soil and sterile containers. Buying a mixture labeled for starting seeds, using finely milled peatmoss, or heating moist soil in the oven to 160° F for thirty minutes gives the best results. Commercial seed-growing media are formulated for a balance between water retention and air circulation. Rinsing flats with a disinfectant reduces contamination.

90 | If you are going to start perennial seedlings indoors, harden them off slowly in the spring by reducing the temperature and increasing the amount of light they receive. Put them outside in a sheltered spot—preferably near the back door—and keep an eye on them. Slowly let them dry out a little more in between watering. Give them small but regular amounts of

fertilizer. Slowly they will respond and grow.

---

91 **Biennials can be confusing.** A true biennial flowers during its second year and dies after that. Infrequently some biennials grow like tender perennials and flower a third and even a fourth year. Typically hollyhocks are biennials, but some varieties grow as annuals, some grow as perennials, and some grow as biennials but flower their first year from seed. Parsley is also a biennial, but the second year only a few leaves and a flowering head appear. This makes its second year relatively useless. *Viola cornuta* behaves like an annual, blooming after its first year. Sweet William (*Dianthus barbata*) may survive as a perennial for several years.

---

92 **Starting seeds of biennials every year insures a consistent display of flowers.** Some seeds, like parsley, won't overwinter and must be started each year from fresh seed. Parsley seed is particularly short-lived while hollyhock seed is winter-hardy and long-lived.

Planting

| 93 | Whether using seeds or transplants, water the bed before planting. A dry bed easily desiccates anything put into it. Moist soil provides an environment into which roots move quickly. Even waiting the minutes or hours it would take to water the bed after planting gives dry soil plenty of time to draw water from tender roots. After planting, transplants need a thorough watering to seal any large airspaces which would dry out roots. Firm the soil around the roots of newly set-in plants. A cloudy day or a late afternoon gives an environment that slows the drying of the plant.

| 94 | Cut vertically around the root ball of transplants that have thick, matted roots. Roots circling inside the pot or that completely fill the pot like dreadlocks need redirecting to knit into the soil.

Roots grow in the direction they are pointing. When roots curl around and around the pot, their growth rate and vigor decline. Only constant watering in the garden center maintains them. Pruning the roots with three to five vertical cuts around the root ball stimulates the roots to form new branches and head into the surrounding soil. Gently unravel less matted root balls to encourage them to spread out in the soil.

| 95 | **Make the hole large enough for the roots to spread out.** |

Roots that are cramped when first planted will stay that way. Amend the soil before planting. Adding enough compost, peat moss, or sand to raise the bed slightly helps to improve drainage. To the soil that you put back into the hole, add about one-third to one-half peat moss or compost.

| 96 | **Encourage the roots to make the transition from the soil** |

mix in the pot to the soil in the ground. If the plant is simply plunked out of the pot into a hole in the garden, chances are slim that its roots will leave the light peaty mix of most container soils. Gently pull the roots away from the root ball and point them in the right direction. Make a transition band of soil in the hole by adding peat moss, compost, and perhaps sand to the hole.

| 97 | **When planting any perennial, let water run into the** **hole as you put the soil mix back in.** Not adding enough water at the time the transplant is planted persists as a common planting error. The plant in the new soil may even seem soupy. Once you have planted and watered thoroughly, wait until the soil and the plant show signs of needing water before watering again. Unless the plant shows stress by wilting, 1 to 2 inches of water per week should be enough.

| 98 | **Plant aggressive perennials** **like many mints, grasses like** **the plain Miscanthus sinensis, gooseneck and yellow loosestrife (*Lysimachia clethroides* and *L. punctata*), and the 'Silver Queen'**

and 'Silver King' *Artemisia ludoviciana* in 5- to 10-gallon plastic buckets buried with the bottoms cut out. The sides of the buckets prevent the roots or rhizomes from spreading out. This method helps keep track of plants like poppies whose foliage dies back after flowering. Large clay drainage tiles or 55-gallon plastic barrels buried on end would serve the same purpose for larger plants or planting areas. Leave about 1 or 2 inches out of the soil to help mark the spot where they are buried.

99 For those who dig and move spring-flowering bulbs in the fall, finding them is often the biggest problem. Their foliage dies back leaving virtually no trace. The technique of weaving grape hyacinths around clumps of small spring-flowering bulbs to mark their spot works well. The grape hyacinth leaves last all summer or, if they die back, they regrow in the fall. The clear blue of the most popular variety makes it an excellent companion for the warm tones of most spring bulbs.

Starting New Beds

| 100 | **Starting a new garden requires killing or removing the grass.** Turning grass over rarely eliminates it from the garden. Some of my gardening friends advocate tilling the ground over again after a period of a few weeks, but my tilled ground seems to sprout grasses and weeds for ages. When grasses do sprout from rhizomes in the garden, grass becomes very invasive. A new grass plant will sprout from every sprig or piece of rhizome. Spading up the turf or using a sod stripper is one way to avoid pulling grass out of the garden for years.

| 101 | **Using a sod stripper is one of the fastest ways to remove sod for a new bed.** A sod stripper has a blade that undercuts the roots of the turf so that it can be rolled up or taken off in chunks. I have used a stripper that is pushed like a non-motorized lawn mower and one that has a gasoline engine. They both

work well, but the motorized one is easier and faster to use.

| 102 | A smothering mulch is one method of starting a new bed. Since I have seen a dandelion squeeze through 8 inches of mushroom compost, I often sense some weeds need heavy artillery! Thick layers of newspaper covered with sand and/or organic matter over the proposed garden should decompose enough to be tilled within a year. (An unfolded section of a Sunday edition with roughly twenty pages will act as a heavy-duty barrier and still be organic.)

| 103 | Choose a method of bed edging to control encroaching grass. For a hand-edged bed, use a flat spade or special edging tool to cut an edge around the garden. Slice a 30°- angled space between the bed and the lawn. Make the bottom of the wedge about 6 inches deep. Going around the beds once or twice a year keeps the "run in" weeds at bay.

104 Any commercial edging materials should be sold with a **stake that anchors the edging below the frost line.** If they stayed in the ground, these strips might keep out the weeds. Most come without any way to anchor them. Since in much of the Midwest the ground freezes between 2 and 3 feet deep, the edging pops out of the ground. When edging is sold with anchoring stakes, most of these stakes are only 6 to 12 inches long. Any stake that does not reach below the frost line or that is not anchored horizontally will not hold the edging into the ground.

105 Many types of 4- to 6-inch edging will lift out — unless you stake it. Drive a 9-inch nail or stake horizontally through black plastic edging about halfway down from the top. (When put directly into the ground, edging with the inexpensive, black plastic strips quickly becomes a nightmare. The coils of plastic unwind neatly at the edge of the bed separating it from the lawn, but, with the push of the heaving ground, pop out in the spring.)

106 To anchor an edging into the ground, a flexible stake can be bent over the top surface of the edging, pushed down the side into the ground, and then bent horizontally out into the soil. When the edging is put into the ground, this horizontal anchor slows the creep of the edging toward the surface and out of the ground entirely. Any stake driven at an angle into the soil holds the edging more securely than does one pounded straight down in line with the edging.

107 For constructing a raised bed or a retaining wall (properly installed), you can use wood, bricks, flagstone, collected boulders, or chunks of discarded concrete to make effective beds. A footing below grade level, in most cases below the frost line, keeps the wall from tumbling. Anchor taller wood retaining walls with an extension of wall into the bank. A netting material layered horizontally into the bank and pinned with stakes can help hold a wall in place.

| 108 | Whether a wall is three bricks high or thirty bricks high, it should angle slightly backward into the bank. Although the pitch should be imperceptible, it will slow forward expansion as the ground freezes behind it. A series of shorter walls 3 to 4 feet high and terraced at 4-foot intervals produces the most stable retaining wall. The 4-foot surface between the walls serves as an excellent planting bed.

GROWING PERENNIALS

❀ ❀ ❀

Light

109 In order to produce flowers, all perennials need adequate light. If flowering slacks off and plants grow spindly or leggy, suspect low light in relation to the temperature as the problem. Warm temperatures stimulate growth, but without adequate light the plants look emaciated. When plants fall over instead of having a sturdy, upright growth, that is another signal of poor light and high temperatures.

| 110 | Trees and shrubs are both an asset and a hardship. Trees cool and insulate the house and garden. Many homes built on the site of old fields wait years for their benefit. But too much shade prevents all summer-flowering perennials from blooming. In the middle of the summer, a densely shaded, woodland floor has almost no growth. A very shady yard may be limited to spring-flowering bulbs and early wildflowers. A shady yard requires careful placement of beds to catch the maximum amount of light.

| 111 | Many gardeners fail when they try to grow plants in the shade that they have seen and admired growing in the sun. Here are some that I have seen doing well in light shade or filtered sun:

Anemone (*A. 'Robustissima'*)
Beebalm (*Monarda*)
Bellflower (*Campanula*)
Bluebells (*Mertensia*)
Columbine (*Aquilegia*)
Coral Bells (*Heuchera*)
Daylily (*Hemerocallis*)
False Solomon's seal (*Smilacina*)
Geranium (*Geranium*)

Lungwort (*Pulmonaria*)
Meadow sweet (*Filipendula*)
Monkshood (*Aconitum*)
Phlox species
Solomon's seal (*Polygonatum*)
Sundrops (*Oenothera*)
Turtlehead (*Chelone*)
Violet (*Viola*)

112 If your soil is a moist, rich humus loam with some shade or filtered light, become acquainted with some of these perennials:

Astilbe —very moist
Black snakeroot (*Cimicifuga*)
Bleeding Heart (*Dicentra*)
Bloodroot (*Sanguinaria*)
Brunnera —very moist
Cardinal flower (*Lobelia*) —very moist
Celandine poppy (*Stylophorum*)
Dutchman's Breeches (*Dicentra*)
Foamflower (*Tiarella*)
Forget-me-not (*Myosotis*)
Foxglove (*Digitalis*)
Hardy begonia (*Begonia gradis*)
Lenten & Christmas rose (*Helleborus*)
Leopard's bane (*Doronicum*)
Ligularia —very moist

Primrose (*Primula*)
Spring beauty (*Claytonia*)
Squirrel Corn (*Dicentra*)
Trillium
Yellow corydalis (*Corydalis*)

Although their growing requirements may look demanding, these
perennials grow in many gardens in
shade or filtered light and without
amended soil. Older neighborhoods
with shady overgrown lots can ac-
commodate these prizes rather easily.

| 113 | Yarrow (*Achillea* sp.) grows
vigorously throughout the
Midwest. The various cultivars
sport lacy leaves and long-lasting
flowers. I particularly like the popular pale yellow 'Moonshine' whose
gray-green foliage softly stands out
in the midsummer garden. Its compact size makes it suitable in gardens
that cannot hold the stately *Achillea*
x 'Coronation Gold' or its taller rel-
ative *Achillea filipendulina*. It does
best in well-drained soil and full sun.
Like many sun-loving plants, in
lower than optimum light, it flops
over.

Water

114 **Provide enough water to your plants to reach their entire root systems.** The general 1 inch of water per week given all at once soaks into good garden loam to a depth of about 8 inches. Any amount less than that leaves the lowest part of the root system dry. Deep watering less often is more beneficial to the garden than frequent shallow watering. Watering the top few inches, even frequently, encourages only the roots at the top layer to grow. In soil containing lots of clay, water penetrates less deeply. In sandy soil it penetrates deeper.

115 **Really well-drained soil is critical for growing many sought-after perennials.** The following lovelies are well-known for their aversion to "wet feet." This is the label given to plants whose roots prefer very well-drained sites. Many withstand drought better than other perennials. They must not sit in water or become waterlogged.
Asiatic lilies (*Lilium*)

Baby's breath (*Gypsophila*)
Basket-of-gold (*Aurinia*)
Bearded iris
Bearded tongue (*Penstemon* sp.)
Blanket flower (*Gaillardia*)
Butterfly weed (*Asclepias tuberosa*)
Candytuft (*Iberis*)
Coneflower (*Rudbeckia*)
Coreopsis
Creeping phlox (*Phlox subulata*)
Euphorbia
Maltese cross (*Lychnis chalcedonica*)
Miscanthus 'Gracillimus'
Perennial flax (*Linum perenne*)
Perennial salvia
Purple coneflower (*Echinacea*)
Red hot poker (*Kniphofia uvaria*)
Snow-in-summer (*Cerastium*)

Working extra sand into the spots where the above perennials are planted helps them survive. Check the section on soils for other tips.

116 The bearded iris also grows best in well-drained soil. Any soil that remains waterlogged or drains slowly (as do heavy clay soils) puts stress on the plant. These less vigorous plants suffer more borer damage than do plants in well-

drained soils. One tip for growing iris in clay loam soil: make sure the rhizome is not totally covered by soil. Leaving as much as one-third of the rhizome showing above the ground produces no ill effects in my garden and is crucial to reducing rot.

117 **In a small area, for three mum plants change an area 3 feet by 3 feet to a depth of 18 to 20 inches.** Part of this can be above ground. In that way the raised garden bed gets additional surface drainage. Some gardeners totally change the soil. A few plants such as chrysanthemums, *Achillea*, *Asclepias*, oriental poppies, and *Dianthus* rot in heavy, soggy subsoil. The raised bed avoids the sunken garden effect in which the plants are somewhat hidden from view as well as drowned.

118 **Astilbe are beautiful with their bright, feathery plumes from mid- to late summer.** Often cultural notes will direct these to the shady spots in the garden. Actually, the shade helps reduce their water loss. They are water-hungry and without it their reticulated leaves begin to turn brown at the edges. Planting these in a shady spot that also happened to be dry would not be doing this plant any favors. As a matter of fact with the midwestern heat, keep it rather wet. *Brunnera*, bleeding heart (*Dicentra*), forget-me-not (*Myosotis*), cardinal flower (*Lobelia*), and *Ligularia* all prefer and thrive in wet conditions.

119 **Hydrogel products help hold water in the soil for newly planted plants.** For about the first 3 times they are soaked, the polyacrylamide granules absorb 20 times their weight in water. They won't hold extra water on the fourth watering. They expand, looking like tiny slimy chunks of clear Jell-O. The slippery nature of the product makes it hard to work with when wet. It offers only an initial advantage for permanent plantings and containers, not for soil that is cultivated frequently or that is poorly drained.

120 Accurate and adequate watering often means the difference between a garden that survives and one that doesn't. Many companies offer in-ground watering systems. Using a system like this saves a lot of personal energy, but make sure it uses water economically as well. Don't install a system that delivers one rate of water to your entire property. You should be able to intervene easily and to adjust the watering schedule to fit the needs of the plants. Each bed should be on a separate set of commands and should also be integrated with the entire property.

121 Keeping water from leaf surfaces late in the day slows the spread of waterborne diseases. With the cooling of evening temperatures, water evaporates more slowly from the leaves. The moisture speeds the spread of a wide range of bacterial and fungal diseases. High humidity further aggravates the situation. Brown or black spots on the leaves and leaves covered with a white powdery coating are the signs of these diseases.

122 If left on top of the soil, sphagnum peat moss dries into an impenetrable mat. Water easily runs off the top of the dried material. Work peat moss into the soil with a small trowel or garden spade. Partially decomposed peat moss, often labeled as organic peat, is darker in color and takes up water more easily than the lighter brown surface moss.

123 Watering with a soaker or trickle-type hose tends to discourage diseases like black spot and mildew. Foliage that remains wet, particularly at night, increases the likelihood that the plant will become affected with these problems. Nights when the dew is thick and days when the air is humid are hard enough on most garden plants without adding water to the leaves. Water the ground directly when possible.

124 Soaker hoses made of black, porous plastic, which seems to sweat water, do not wet the leaves. With this type of hose only a band of soil roughly 2 feet wide receives water directly. To cover the entire bed, shift the hose periodically during watering. Don't guess how much water your plant is getting. Check the soil and avoid wasting water as well as under-watering plants.

| 125 | Cover soaker-type hoses with a thin layer of soil, compost, or wood chips. A thin layer shades the hoses from U.V. light and helps them last longer. They will still deliver water efficiently but when lightly covered, the black hoses will not absorb as much heat or disintegrate as rapidly from exposure to the light.

| 126 | For the best results — particularly when using a sprinkler — water early in the day. The plant uses more water during the day so the water won't just sit around on the leaves causing problems. Overhead watering in midday will not necessarily burn plant tissue, but during that time evaporation will be highest. When you water in the late

afternoon during humid weather, the water stands on the leaves overnight, which promotes diseases. Fungi and bacteria can grow without light but need high humidity during warm or cool weather.

127 **Use a rain gauge to keep track of when and how much to water.** After a rain the local news stations usually report the amount. But unless you live next to the weather station, having a rain gauge is the only way to tell how much water your yard got. Rainfall amounts vary widely over a very short distance. Strange as it sounds, a rain gauge is a fascinating device. Walking out and checking the water your garden has collected becomes a ritual that will bind you to the needs of the soil. It is a conduit for tuning in to the environment.

Weeds

128 **Work to extract weeds before they flower and set seed.** Pulling a weed after it sets seed is like closing the barn door after the cows are out. You'll have to round up all the seedlings. Weeds in a garden, besides being unsightly, steal nutrients and water and help transmit insects and disease. A weed-free garden means continual involvement. The most carefree garden is a garden that is weeded regularly. Even experienced gardeners pull weeds every time they walk through the garden. Taking out weeds in small amounts on a regular basis keeps weeding simple.

129 As a rule, each hour spent in the garden weeding in the spring is worth two later in the summer. The moist, soft, spring soil gives up the weeds more easily and more completely than the drier summer soil. Seedling weeds come out faster and in their entirety, whereas older weeds have a tighter hold. But weed seeds sprout all summer long. Oxalis or wood sorrel is a winter annual, which means it sprouts from seed in the late summer, lives over the winter, and dies in the spring. For this reason although I personally find spring weeding much more enjoyable than hot, late summer weeding, gardening takes year-round attention.

130 **Learn to distinguish between the attractive, easy to control "invaders" and the troublesome, impossible to get rid of "weeds."** Of course any plant growing where you don't want it is a "weed," but some plants put a grip on a garden that seems impossible to break. For me that's a real weed. Buy a good reference manual. Take a class in weed identification from an extension class, botanic garden, or arboretum in your area. Remember, one person's wandering wonder is another persons obnoxious weed!

131 **Low-growing plants with shallow surface roots can be weeding nightmares.** *Phlox subulata,* creeping phlox, edges many gardens and rock walls. However, rhizome grass growing into a planting destroys it. The tightly woven grass roots and underground stems hold the ground better than the shallow-rooted perennials. Weeding out the grass pulls out the phlox. Growing phlox slightly above the level of the lawn or in a bed with a good edging slows the invasion of turf grass. And the looser the soil, the easier the weeding.

132 In wet areas avoid common purple loosestrife (*Lythrum salicaria*). By being extremely aggressive it can take over wetlands. The resulting area is a monoculture with the range of the many diverse native plants squeezed out. In some states it is illegal to grow it. Champion only hybrids of lythrum, which do not readily produce seedling. Check with your state's conservation district or your cooperative extension service.

133 My own weed nemesis list includes *Convolvulus arvensis* (field bindweed), *Tovara virginianum* (jumpseed), *Viola papilionacea* (common blue violet), *Alliaria officinalis* (garlic mustard), and *Glechoma hederacea* (ground ivy or creeping Charlie). I know people and books that rate most of these as useful plants! But believe

me, if they rank among the invaders in your garden, you will find them formidable adversaries. Jumpseed, common blue violet, and garlic mustard seeds germinate everywhere. The deep roots of field bindweed travel underground for yards, sprouting shoots along the way. Creeping Charlie grows from the smallest chunk of stem left in the garden and grows so quickly, I know you could see it spread and grow if you sat still very long.

| 134 | In a bed blended with many different plants, grow only grasses or other plants that form clumps. Avoid those that spread aggressively by rhizomes. Rhizomes are underground stems that often weave a tight fabric of growth. They are wonderful for holding ground. Isolate these tough plants where other things won't grow or where they can be kept in bounds by a mower or some other barrier. A few common rhizomatous growers include artemisia, maiden grass (*Miscanthus sinesis*), rose yarrow (*Achillea rosea*), creeping bellflower (*Campanula*

rapunculoides), and ladybells (*Adenophora confusa*).

135 Beware: some flowering plants grown as ground covers are impossible to get rid of. Bishop's weed (*Aegopodium podagraria*) sprouts from the smallest bit of stem left in the soil. It will live for years and survive being covered, smothered, and dug! Lily-of-the-valley (*Convallaria majalis*) travels. I have seen it pop up in the cracks of a driveway and even come up on the other side. It is fragrant, beautiful, and often too vigorous to be included in mixed border. Creeping Jenny (*Lysimachia nummularia*) as a low-growing plant can escape into the moist areas of your lawn with great vigor. I have heard of Bugleweed (*Ajuga*) traveling into a lawn that was henceforth referred to as "Buglelawn."

136 Tree and shrub seedlings rank among the worst garden weeds. If woody plant seedlings grow more than a year in the garden, digging them out becomes an operation in miniature stump removal. And like the worst those of the perennial herbaceous weeds, roots left in the ground often grow new shoots. Learn to identify them and pull them as tiny seedlings. Common and glossy buckthorn (*Rhamnus cathartica* and *R. frangula*), amur and other shrub honeysuckles (*Lonicera maackii, L. tatarica,* etc.), common mulberry (*Morus alba*), boxelder (*Acer negundo*), and Siberian elm (*Ulmus pumila*) are the most aggressive in my area. Pin or wild red cherry and choke cherry (*Prunus pensylvanica* and *P. virginiana*) along with the hawthorns (*Crataegus* sp.) also invade open gardens for a woody takeover.

---

137 Weeds do not respect property lines; they will brazenly travel from your neighbor's yard to yours. Underground rhizomes of grasses and perennial weeds like field bindweed or creeping Charlie attest to the notion that "Good fences make good neighbors." Finding a barrier to keep them out improves relations considerably. One technique is to bury a strip of plastic sheeting vertically along the edge of the property. A piece about 8 inches wide and 6 mm thick that runs the length of the garden will thwart most weedy invaders.

138 Unless you have a lot of money or a lot of time or both, don't plan a large garden that will take hours to maintain. I don't mean you must be retired or wealthy, but understand the commitment involved. Start small and enlarge your garden as your enthusiasm grows.

Additional Climate Concerns

139 Don't be discouraged when a plant you've had for years suddenly and for no apparent reason dies. Plants like aquilegia, achillea, feverfew, monarda, or coreopsis seem so hardy, then one spring they're gone. A plant like portulaca, cleome, or cosmos may reseed faithfully year after year — then one year, nothing. Different sets or sequences of weather conditions favor different plants. As growing trees increase the shade, the garden evolves and changes. Successful gardens are built slowly over the years by adding and subtracting, by interacting with the natural world.

140 The maximum cold temperatures alone do not dictate which plants will survive in the northern versus the southern range of the Midwest. Often prolonged hot, dry periods cause plants to decline or die during the summer. The texture, structure, and pH of the soil determine which plants thrive. Rapid-draining soils are critical to members of the genus *Dianthus* as much as thicker richer soils enhance the vigor of *Paeonia*.

141 Plants that put on a burst of growth in the fall often don't survive the winter. Many delicate plants like primroses suffer stress and slow their growth during the hottest part of the summer. Later, during the cooler fall weather, they

often put out a flush of succulent growth. Most plants tend to go dormant as winter approaches. Unfortunately, the new, rapidly growing tissues usually die back. The reserve of carbohydrates in the root system dissipates and the entire plant perishes in the cold.

142 **In those winters when the ground freezes very early, and especially right after several days or weeks of heavy rain, the root systems of many shallow-rooted plants die.** Soil saturated with water freezes, tearing the roots apart. The extra water does not become a reservoir for later use; it is a destructive force that causes the plant to lose its root system. Putting the plant in a well-drained site is the only possible prevention for such disaster.

143 **The best winter for your garden is one in which the ground freezes slowly and then is blanketed by a thick covering of snow that lasts all winter.** A foot or two of snow is the best insulation

against swings in temperature. Soil temperature changes slowly under a good covering of snow. The slower the ground freezes and warms, the better chance shallow-rooted plants have to survive.

144 In this uncertain climate and difficult soil, don't give up on a plant if it dies. If you really like a certain plant, try to grow it at least three more times. Each time, change the spot in which you are growing it. Amend the soil more carefully. Make sure the plant has adequate moisture on a regular basis. Often it takes just the right combination of growing conditions to get a plant established.

145 Hosta are one of the most sensitive perennials to a late spring frost. Even a light frost blanketing the fully opened leaves causes them to die. Plants do put out a new flush of growth but it is slow in coming. Given a frost in mid- to late May, plants that have emerged completely will take about three to four weeks to recover. Leaves that are hit by frost while they are still emerging and are rolled tightly in a bud don't suffer to the same extent.

146 In the central and southern areas of the Midwest, the high humidity carries disease in almost every droplet of water vapor. A thick canopy of shade may act as a lid, slowing the movement of air around the garden. I've had powdery mildew cover monarda in an area of "dead air" only to be totally absent on nearby plants growing in a windier spot. Either put a susceptible plant where air moves much more freely or prune trees to bring in some light and fresh air.

147 If possible, buy perennial plants that have grown for generations from local stock. Plants of the same species vary genetically. Sometimes natural genetic variation within a single species produces differences that can be seen. Naturally occurring variation leads to rather striking differences or to subtle genetic distinctions. A harsh environment may be the selecting

agent for plants that are slightly more genetically rugged than plants grown in environments with less climatic stress. If the nurseries in harsh climates develop their own seed stock, the plants may be naturally selected for that region. On the other hand, just buying seeds and planting them in a rough climate won't impart any hardiness to the seedlings.

| 148 | **Every flowering season in the Midwest produces a new view of the garden.** A slight change in the weather—cool, hot, dry, wet—often shifts flowering a week or two one way or the other. A hot spring with one heavy rain may ruin the peonies as they hit their peak. A friend tells me that there is an unwritten natural law that every spring when the double peonies bloom, at least one heavy wind and rain storm will beat them to the ground. The variability of seasons gives different plants a chance to overlap. A Midwest garden rarely looks the same two years in a row. Enjoy!

PROBLEMS WITH ANIMALS

❀ ❀ ❀

| 149 | Diatomaceous earth makes a good mulch for hosta and other plants plagued by slugs because the earth works to slow the movement of slugs. The sharp-edged skeletons of diatoms, little single-celled sea creatures, are an unwelcome ground cover for the soft underbellies of mollusks as well as caterpillars. Reapply the diatomaceous earth after a rain, and do not inhale the dust.

150 Digging, dividing, and disinfecting iris rhizomes remains a time-honored method of controlling iris borer. The iris borer devastates stands of bearded iris grown in waterlogged soil. Iris put into unsuitable growing conditions suffer from this most devastating of all iris problems. Although several species of iris grow in wet soils along the banks of ponds and lakes, the bearded grow best in very well-drained soils. Siberian iris, which are also common in midwestern gardens, will tolerate more water, making them less likely to become infested with the iris borer. Digging and dividing iris is usually done in July, well after flowering and with enough growing season left to allow vigorous new root systems to develop.

151 The twisted paths made by a leaf miner as it tunnels through the middle layer of the leaf disfigures columbine foliage. Usually the plant withstands the attack. I see it every year on all the cultivars but not usually on the native species *Aquilegia canadensis*. The colorful va-

rieties available in the hybrid cultivars seem more prone to suffer in
poorly drained clay soil. Columbine
are usually short-lived and need to
be started regularly from seed.

| 152 | **Wild things running and fly-
ing through the garden can
be both a delight and a dilemma.**
One owner will buy corn for squirrels to feast on during the winter.
Meanwhile a neighbor plots all winter to rid the garden of varmints. In
some areas chipmunks, ground
squirrels, and some species of mice
are protected. Before constructing
elaborate traps or an electric fence,
check with your local game warden
or community officials to determine
if any restrictions on animals or control methods apply.

| 153 | **Discourage small rodents
from nesting in the perennial beds by waiting until the
ground freezes to finish the winter
mulching.** If your soil drains slowly,
covering the bed too early may result
in rotting the crowns of the plants.
Rodents may find the early cover

suits them as they munch through the still-green stems. However, leaves naturally cover woodland gardens long before a hard freeze with no ill effect. Timing the winter mulch depends on what you are covering, how well your soil drains, how serious your rodent problem is, and how well you are able to work in really cold weather!

154 **To deter rabbits try dusting baby powder or blood meal around the emerging plants.** Reapply the powder after a heavy dew or rain. Regardless, a fresh dose of powder every seven to ten days should discourage rabbits. Keep up the regime until the plant gets too large or old to be of interest to the rabbits. I personally favor my effective guard cat.

155 **Mice and chipmunks have a taste for the tender little buds of seedlings far more than for the tougher growth of second- or third-year plants.** To protect seedlings from small rodents, cover them with a tent of small-mesh screening.

If space allows, dig the little pots holding the seedlings into a protected spot in the garden for the winter.

Deer

| 156 | Excluding deer from a midwestern garden is an art form. The shortest open fence that will keep deer out without electricity or elaborate barricading is 8 feet. Some deer are even able to jump an 8-foot fence! Contrary to popular opinion, really enterprising deer may jump a solid 5- or 6-foot fence. Besides, a solid fence casts shade. Winding 3-foot chicken wire in a maze throughout the garden, keeps out deer. Deer aren't very good at mazes.

| 157 | Place several large (3-foot by 5-foot) loose cylinders of chicken wire on their sides in and around the garden. Such a maze will usually veer the deer to another path. This system works for a gardening friend of mine who has a large garden in the country, where directing

the deer toward an alternate route seems to do the trick. In the Midwest, discouraging deer can be an obsession!

158 **A very pungent soap with a strong odor, such as Dial soap, puts deer off the scent!** A half bar hung 3 feet from the ground every 6 feet around the garden works. Using a soap with an herbal scent doesn't work, and soaps that dissolve quickly don't last long enough to be effective. Also, if any bar in the chain surrounding the garden is lost, deer quickly find the opening and enter there, so the soap system must be a tightly monitored one.

159 **I've heard human hair in pantyhose hung up in the garden holds deer at bay for a little while, as do some commercial repellents.** Hair and many repellents work until the material oxidizes. Then the scent is lost. On warm days this can take less than twelve hours. You'd have to have access to lots of hair for this technique to work for long!

160 The simplicity of the Minnesota Zaps electric fence is elegant. One line of electric wire 4 feet high surrounds the garden. Every 3 to 4 feet, a piece of aluminum foil folded over the wire hides a smelly, thick smear of peanut butter. Cloth tape on the inside of the foil holds the bait in place. When lured to the spot by the smell of peanut butter, the deer receives a harmless but very discouraging shock.

161 A typical electric deer fence has electric wires that are held out from the fence by insulators. The 7-wire slant fence has wires at roughly 1-foot intervals along a fence that angles out from the garden at 45°.

162 Another inventive system for an electric fence uses two short fences to form a type of barricade. One fence is 4 feet tall with 2 wires—one 6 inches from the bottom to keep smaller animals out and one near the top. The second fence—placed 4 feet in front of the first fence — is 2½ feet tall with an electric wire at the top.

163 If they are used according to the label directions, commercial repellents are a useful tool in the ongoing struggle to keep deer out of the midwestern garden. Soak rags with these liquids and hang them in your garden at about 3 to 4 feet. (At the level of the plants you are protecting!) As the scent wears off, the repellent must be reapplied. Place rags at intervals no greater than 6 feet. Where any repellent spills on the ground, plants die back.

CARING
FOR YOUR
GARDEN
THROUGH
THE
SEASONS

❀ ❀ ❀

| 164 | Keep a garden diary — either a simple or an elaborate one. For the simple version, keep receipts for the plants you buy and tape them in a notebook. That will give you some idea of what you bought and when. But logging each plant — when it begins to grow, to flower,

and to fade—provides the most interesting and accurate record of your garden. This together with an instant photo of the flower will help you with next winter's planning. Making a sketch of your garden showing where each plant is located helps you maintain balance and rhythm from one year to the next.

165 **Trying out plants remains the best way to find out how they grow. Experience is the best teacher.** When the cultural information specifies well-drained, light shade, look for three spots in your garden that fit that description. It is likely that each spot will be different with regard to light, air circulation, or soil. Small microclimates exist in the garden that vary enough to grow considerably different plants. Logging performance over several years gives the best information for your garden.

166 **A plant that is healthy and that is grown with the best cultural techniques suffers less from diseases and insects than do**

plants under stressful growing conditions. Although plants don't have a direct correlation to an immune system, vigorous plants are less likely to have disease and insect problems than plants growing poorly. Sometimes a plant is infected with a fungal disease, but healthy plant growth keeps the problem in check. Only a few lesions or some streaking appear on the leaves. Then if the weather puts an infected plant in a weakened condition, a disease present in the plant for a few hours to several years may all of a sudden kill leaves, stems, roots—even the entire plant.

| 167 | **Try labeling plants by writing with waterproof markers on pieces of masonite cut as tags, drilled with a hole, and looped with a piece of wire.** Labeling plants |

that are dormant helps to identify areas where foliage dies back to the ground. Digging into an area of dormant spring-flowering bulbs often slices the bulbs in two. Even walking on the dormant tops of *Trillium* sp. kills the next year's shoots. By September the tips lie hidden, waiting for spring. Even in the spring, not all plants emerge from the ground at the same time. Butterfly weed (*Asclepias tuberosa*) and balloon flower (*Platycodon grandiflorus*) come up long after the rest of the garden. An unlabeled spot might easily be dug up.

168 Although many professionals say, "Prune when the saw is sharp," following a few guidelines gives good results. If the plant blooms in April, May, or early June, prune before the fourth of July. If the plant blooms in late June or July, prune in March or April before the buds break. For the early bloomers, this schedule gives you a chance to see the blooms before pruning.

169 If you cut many dwarf flowering shrubs to the ground every three or four years, they will flower as if they were vigorous, newly planted specimens. Vigorous shrubs will add beauty to your flower garden. The technique is called rejuvenation pruning. Low-growing spireas commonly benefit from this. Any time up to midsummer is suitable for this pruning. Since the plant goes dormant before winter, cutting it in late summer or early fall may kill it.

---

170 Some woody plants like blue-mist shrub (*Caryopteris*), butterfly-bush (*Buddleia*), and some clematis species die back to the ground each year. They essentially grow as herbaceous perennials. They receive "cut-back" pruning every spring and grow new shoots from near the ground. Given this special treatment, they are lovely additions to the garden.

---

171 The grasslands of the Midwest have been maintained for thousands of years by fire. The area has a characteristic low rainfall that favors the deep roots of grasses and their companion forbs. Those rains that do soak the regions often come with violent thunder and lightning storms. Fire sweeping across the open expanses of grasses kills the small trees and nonprairie herbs. Burning a prairie garden in late winter or very early spring remains one of the best ways to promote the growth of prairie species. Although using a rolled newspaper as a small torch works well to burn the stems, check with your fire department for burning regulations and restrictions in your area.

| 172 | Burning the prairie garden encourages growth by eliminating competing plants that die in the fire and by stimulating the prairie plants themselves. Burning the dead, dried stems encourages vigourous new growth. I'm not sure why cutting the plant back won't work as well, except that new stem buds are formed just below the cut. If this is above ground, fewer new stems sprout—probably because the top buds sprout quickly, suppressing further side-bud growth. It is also likely that burning the abundant dry stems and leaves adds potassium to the soil, boosting plant growth. Regardless of the exact technical mechanism, prairie plants that are burned grow more vigorously than ones that are not. Do not burn a prairie bed without first checking

local ordinances and with your fire department.

173 **If you are timid about dividing perennials for fear of killing them, start with a vigorous, old stand of hosta.** A shovel or sharp-edged spade thrust into the center of a clump of hosta neatly divides the plant. Each hosta must have a crown or growing point attached to a piece of thick root. Dividing the clump into single crown pieces produces many small plants, but remember: the smaller the piece the slower the recovery. A single crown division may take two to four years to grow into a full lush stand.

174 **Although some perennials rarely if ever need to be divided, others depend on division to keep them vigorous.** A few of these include yarrow—particularly the yellow ones (*Achillea*), aster, astilbe, boltonia, campanula, chrysanthemum, leopard's bane (*Doronicum*), fleabane (*Erigeron*), perennial sunflower (*Helianthus*), phlox, evening primrose (*Oenothera*), iris, heliopsis, monarda, goldenrod (*Solidago*), salvia, stokes aster (*Stokesia*), and veronica. Note when the center of the clump begins to die, when the flowers are small or few, and when the flowering time seems shorter than usual. These are some signs that the plants need division.

| 175 | Almost any plant can be dug, divided, and replanted but some are certainly more difficult than others. Among the plants that do not transplant well or easily are milkweeds (*Asclepias*), *Anemone japonica*, false blue indigo (*Baptisia*), gas plant (*Dictamnus*), globe thistle (*Echinops*), sea holly (*Eryngium*), baby's breath (*Gypsophila*), statice (*Limonium*), lupines (*Lupinus*), peony (*Paeonia*), poppies (*Papaver*), balloon flower (*Platycodon*), thermopsis, Virginia blue bells (*Mertensia*), and clematis. Although Christmas rose (*Helleborus*) and monkshood (*Aconitum*) share their reputation, one of my gardening friends notes that they hold up well to the procedure. Perhaps this proves once again that gardening is truly experimental.

| 176 | Sometimes division is an artful way to hold in check an aggressive plant. When one clump starts to take over too much of the garden, dig some of it out. If that doesn't work, dig the whole thing out! Some notable assertive plants in midwestern gardens include the genus *Artemesia*—except for 'Silver Mound', which melts out rather consistently—golden Marguerite (*Anthemis*), goldenrod (*Solidago*), beebalm (*Monarda*), false dragonhead (*Physostegia*), and perennial sunflower (*Helianthus*).

| 177 | Dividing some plants is best done with a saw. Thick matted rhizomes of Siberian iris, goat's beard (*Aruncus dioicus*), and maiden grass (*Miscanthus sinesis*) defy division with a spade. Lift the entire plant out by undercutting the roots. When the roots resist division with the sharpest spade, take a saw to the mass. A few shoots along the cut edge may be cut in two, but you'll get the job done successfully and in short order.

178 June is the best month to divide hosta. They are actively growing and the plants quickly begin forming new roots. If they are divided before growth begins, start up is slow. If you wait until late in the summer, the root loss tends to make the broad leaves of the transplanted hosta wilt in the mid-afternoon heat.

179 Cutting off flowers after they bloom is called dead-heading. Although all seed heads are attractive to some people, I think dead-heading daisies, peonies, and liatris improves their appearance. *Coreopsis grandiflora* stands out as one of the more notorious candidates for dead-heading. After the first flush of blooms, it flowers sporadically all summer, leaving dried, dark, dead flowers in its wake. If the plant is not thoroughly and routinely cut back, the dotting of new flowers gets lost among the dying ones.

180 For some plants, cutting off old flowers keeps them blooming longer or even stimulates

a second flush of flowers. Cutting back dame's rocket (*Hesperis*), feverfew (*Chrysanthemum parthenium*), yarrow (*Achillea*), delphinium, phlox, globe thistle (*Echinops*), perennial flax (*Linum*), the veronicas, and perennial salvia nearly to the ground initiates a second cycle of growth. Look at the base of the plant. If new shoots are sprouting at the base of the old, most likely the plant will benefit from cutting out the old, leggy, spent stems. Leaving old foliage standing when fresh, new leaves are at the bottom of the plant defeats the purpose of rejuvenation.

---

181 **To slow the spread of any of the leaf diseases, such as the many leaf spots and rusts, collect all the fallen or diseased leaves and throw them away.** Letting the infected foliage lie on the ground inoculates nearby susceptible plants not already infected. Even if all the plants have the problem, leaving the leaves around will make it worse. If allowed to overwinter under the plant, they can affect next year's foliage.

182 Hollyhocks are subject to one major problem: a rust that puts holes in the leaves and turns them to a rusty color. So prevalent is the problem, I've seen a watercolor of hollyhocks that included the riddled leaves. Some gardeners rip them out from frustration with their diseased appearance, but some creatively use other, shorter plants to hide their ugly lower parts. It seems no matter how the leaves look, riddled with rust as they no doubt become, they come back, bloom, and tower over the garden.

183 After the ground has frozen, clean up the leaves of irises and peonies. Both of these perennials suffer from diseases that overwinter in the dead foliage. Peonies that have leaves streaked with red and buds that dry up unopened are infected with a botrytis fungus. Cut the stems as low to the ground as possible and discard or bury any diseased foliage. This will slow the spread of infections.

Moving Indoors for the Winter

| 184 | Gardeners need to know which plants easily overwinter indoors in pots, which ones are tricky, and which ones to forget.

First any plant brought in from outside will need as much light as you can give it. If that light is artificial, fluorescent light works well. Put the plant no further than 1 foot from the light and leave it on for at least 16 hours a day. The extended exposure helps make up for the lower light intensity.

| 185 | Rosemary does not overwinter in midwestern gardens.

But with some care, it is a small, attractive, woody plant that overwinters indoors. Best results come from growing rosemary in the same pot indoors and out. Rosemary is a heavy water user and is not at all forgiving when you let it dry out. Choose a large enough pot and a soil mix with a generous addition of peat moss to allow at least 3 days between watering. During the summer, burying the pot in the garden slows water loss. Just lift the pot to bring it in the fall. Keep it in the sunniest window and don't let it dry out!

| 186 | **Any plant that overwinters indoors should be kept in the same pot summer and winter.** Transplanting it from open ground to a pot tears off many needed roots. Given the lower light and shorter days of fall, the plant will not be replacing roots as quickly as it would in the spring and summer. Digging them out of the garden and potting them up in September and October doesn't work as well as burying the plant pot and then digging it out.

| 187 | **Roots can, of course, grow out the holes in a pot that is buried in the ground.** To keep the roots *inside* a pot, rotate the pot 360° every once in a while. I suggest that once a week you simply twist the rim of the pot. You might feel the tension of roots anchoring into the ground, and rotating the pot will free the

plant from the ground. The roots will form new branches inside the pot.

188 **When bringing in a plant to overwinter indoors, cut off two-thirds to three-quarters of the plant.** The lush summer growth will usually turn yellow and drop off soon after coming indoors anyway. Besides turning yellow and brown, the summer foliage facing the stress of the hot, dry indoor environment often becomes infested with spider mites. Encourage the plant to put out new growth, better acclimated to the lower indoor light and drier air.

189 **Keep outdoor plants separate from other indoor plants for two to three months.** In this way garden plants are less likely to infest indoor plants with any pests brought in from the outside.

190 The following list may serve as a guide to which annual garden plants to bring in and which ones to start from seed or to buy again in the spring.

Easy to grow indoors
Asparagus fern
Coleus
Geranium
Tuberous begonia
Wax begonia

Need some skill
Impatiens
Lantana
Parsley
Rosemary

Best to forget it
Ageratum
Celosia
Marigold
Nicotiana
Pansy
Petunia
Salvia
Snapdragon
Sweet alyssum
Vinca

| 191 | Rather than digging up entire plants and bringing them indoors, take cuttings, which provide a reliable way to overwinter and increase the number of annual plants in the garden. Coleus, impatiens, and begonias root easily. Cut 3- to 5-inch terminal stems just below a leaf-growing point or node. Remove a few of the lower leaves. Put the shoot into a light-weight, sterile growing media like finely milled mix of peat moss and vermiculite. Keep the cuttings just barely damp to prevent rotting and keep them out of hot, direct light.

| 192 | For cuttings in a particularly arid home environment, place a plastic bag over the top to help slow the evaporation of water. Until the plant grows a root system, it cannot take up water efficiently. Putting the cuttings in a location like direct sun where evaporation is rapid puts an extra stress on the plant. They need bright light but not direct sun. Later, as they begin to grow, take off the bag to prevent the development of mold and fertilize them lightly throughout

the winter. The bag may be left open to let in some air, tied at the bottom with holes punched for ventilation, or secured on two sides like a pup tent.

193 Due to the fungus Pythium, geranium cuttings easily get a disease called "black-leg." The stem at the soil level turns black and slimy. Sterile equipment, a light, well-drained soil mix, and careful cultural technique usually prevent the disease. One friend of mine suggests letting the cuttings sit for three days to dry the cut ends before sticking them in the mix. Another friend roots geraniums in water, but puts less than ¼ inch of water in the jar!

194 For me cuttings taken in spring and planted in the same containers and soil mix used for starting seeds gives consistently high percentages of rooted cuttings. When the plant starts actively growing, many plants form roots more quickly than they do in the fall when they naturally grow less vigorously. Any light, sterile mix works to root cuttings. A well aerated, moist environment is essential. The small plastic trays used to start seeds work well to start cuttings.

195 The floral foam that secures flowers in a flower arrangement makes an excellent material in which to root cuttings. A piece cut to fit a shallow 2- to 3-inch container holds moisture and provides good aeration for the roots. It is difficult to overwater the floral foam, and it dries out uniformly. When the plant has roots, the foam is left on the plant and potted into the container or soil.

196 In order to slow leggy growth, try shaking plants after cutting them back in the fall. Shake the plants vigorously for 5 seconds 2 times a day. Do this morning and night, about 12 hours apart. Shaking mimics windy gusts. As a result the plants don't stretch out as much and are more compact.

| 197 | Sometimes a leggy plant which is receiving just less than the optimum light level can be manipulated to grow full and bushy by cutting it back or pinching off a few inches from the ends. Prune it only before any sign of a clustering of flower buds can be seen. Better too early than too late. Keep an eye on the plant's growth and pinch or cut it before it reaches its normal height. Pinching can help a plant growing indoors as well as a plant in the garden.

| 198 | For overwintering annuals indoors, spider mites and powdery mildew are common problems. Spider mites thrive in hot, dry conditions. Even outdoors, impatiens are sensitive to hot, dry weather. They wilt easily when hit with a hot wind in the late afternoon. When the temperature rises and the humidity falls, a mild spider mite presence becomes a full-blown, webby, mottled mess. Providing plants with plenty of cool temperatures and more humidity reduces the number of mites and allows the plant to grow more vigorously. When you

are trying hard to increase the humidity on plants, powdery mildew may appear on plants like begonias.

CHILDREN AND GARDENING

❀ ❀ ❀

| 199 | Plan a garden with your child in mind and soon your child will be planting a garden of his or her own. When your children are very small, plant spring-flowering bulbs. Start with snowdrops (*Galanthus*)—look for them as soon as the snow melts and the ground *begins* to thaw. Plant crocus, tulips, hyacinths, and daffodils. The joy of those first few springs filled with flowers triggers an interest that is wonderful to watch. Continue with snapdragons—show the child how

they snap! Plant morning glories and watch them race to the top of a fence or trellis. Plant nasturtium and eat the flowers. Involve your children while they are small and you won't be able to keep them out of the garden when they get older!

200 **Let children use their imaginations.** Their garden should be a place where colors can be their own, where form doesn't matter, where even weeds will be tolerated. Have seed catalogs sitting around. Children will be drawn like a magnet. Let them choose seeds to order or plants to buy. My girls introduced me to Shirley poppies, annual asters, bells of Ireland, and variegated iris. Always manage to have a few "extra" seedlings or seeds to add to any open spots in their gardens. These should be some colorful, tried-and-true plants that will flourish — just in case.

INDEX

❋ ❋ ❋

Please note: the numbers below refer to the tips, not the book's pages.

123

124